Northern Swim

Northern Swim

Poems

Maxine Susman

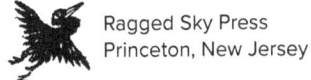

Ragged Sky Press
Princeton, New Jersey

Copyright © 2024 by Maxine Susman

Published by Ragged Sky Press
270 Griggs Drive
Princeton, NJ 08540
raggedsky.com
All Rights Reserved

ISBN: 978-1-933974-58-3

Library of Congress Control Number: 2023951950

This book has been composed in Keplar Standard and Proxima Nova Semibold
Text and cover design by Dirk Rowntree
Cover photo: Acadia National Park by Maxine Susman
Author photo by Miguel Pagliere

Printed on acid-free paper.
Printed in the United States of America

First Edition

for my sister Rita Susman Wolpert, 1949–2020

and for Jay

Contents

One

Snowshoeing at Seventy 3
Bucket List 4
Going All the Way 5
Walk to Trout Pond 6
Northern Swim, Late September 7
Doors to the Pavilion 8
Spring in Manhattan, 1947 9
End of March, 2020 10
My Son Brings Groceries 11
Stay 12
To My Sister in Lockdown 13
Dessert with a Friend on Facetime 14
Tikki Tikki Tembo and the Pandemic 15
'50s Fourth of July 16
Home Phone 17
Ondul 18
The Thing with Feathers 19
Small Change 20
License 21
Sitting Shiva during Pandemic 22

Two

Puppy at the Beach: An Arf Poetica 25
Starfish: Why I'm Not a Painter 26
Anecdotal Footnote to a Natural History of Massachusetts 27
Backyard 28
Eve's Daughter 30
Morning After 32
Picture Tent at the Edge of Camp 33
Belgrade, 1961 34
Open Carry 35
Elsewhere in the News 36
Tableau 37
Yom Kippur in the Catskill Mountains 38
Humanatee 39

Couture   40
Sea Turtle, Cape Cod Bay   41
Mandatory Evacuation   42
Biomass   43
Processional   44
Fox Island Woods   45

Three

New Savage   49
That, Then   50
Sinkhole   51
Rehearsal on the Lawn   52
False Note   53
Mountain Cabin   54
Beaver Territory   55
Good Year for Apples   56
Breton Cake   57
Sweet Potato Pie   58
Florence Griswold's Boardinghouse   59
Of Two Minds   60
Snowstorm   61
The Do Rights at the World of Beers   62
I Don't Know   63
The Gift   64
The Olallieberry   65

Acknowledgments   67
About the Author   69

One

Snowshoeing at Seventy

My first time. A sameness blurs
edges and angles, smoothing them over

shaping black and white, mixing the lines.
Easy to find ourselves

lost here, though buoyed above pitfalls.
Deer, raccoons, chipmunks

we and the dogs leave our tracks too,
your old trooper and my young romper

we plop our plastic platforms down,
bright sun, bright sky, the house

invisible in the distance. A giddiness
to falling, knowing we'll flop

forward or backward sooner or later
like kids bouncing on beds

whoever falls, falls alone and laughing—
can't hold the other to blame,

softening of resentments, letting them go.
Our past missteps hibernate layers down

those brambles, roots, rocks we trip over,
the under-snow creek-flow hot-foot—

—suddenly the huge spruce
laced with snow, pointing in all directions.

Bucket List

What's yours for New Year's? my sister asks,
this last evening of the old one, pink-streaked
above the fields. We're walking the road
past the junk apple trees,
the dogs' noses down, tails up in the ditch,
scenting discoveries—

not the bucket you kick as it kills you
but the one with the song's hopeless hole
that keeps things going for Liza and Henry,
resigned or maybe good-natured nagging,
no solution so no end to the ending,
zigzag circles, sharing a life.

We're just dark shapes, the flashlight busted,
once in a while a car looms—headlights
too close, we back into the brush—
are we, even at near range, visible?

Up the long slope home
she leans more on her walking stick,
taps the center of her forehead
I've got the marker—breast cancer back
after fifteen years' remission—

Anyone anytime, I answer
thinking of deaths in the ending year,
holes in the bucket,
that we all have the marker
tattooed inside us

but I want to give this a happy ending,
the pail by the fireplace filled with kindling.
She leans on her stick, I hold onto luck,
the dogs on their leashes pull us uphill.

Going All the Way

Hey, before you go, want to hug?
We've been working up to this for months
of driveway talks, backyard meals, distanced walks
as today we set out, gives me time to think:
I'll have to tell my husband—
how will it feel, so long since we've done it
maybe I've forgotten how.
(That can't be, you don't forget.)
I challenge, *How many have you done it with?*

My friend ponders and comes clean: Five.
Husband (he doesn't count, always available),
brother, son, two granddaughters. One time each.
My turn: Husband, ditto. Son, ditto.
Brother twice, a month apart so counts for two.
Dog, like my husband, as much as I want.
Dog doesn't count, she says.
Does too. Dog's a person when it comes to hugs.

And the unspoken litany, whose hugs do you miss—
Daughter sister grandkids friends,
that long and growing list (out of reach,
out of touch, gone from this orbiting world).
Gee I don't know—do you think we should—

Worth the risk? Which friends do you trust
out of your sight and how far do you trust them,
whom do you go all the way with
to the end of pandemic and what comes next?
It's an hour later than I said I'd be home—
a little awkward, masks fastened on,
faces turned to opposite sides
we reach for each other and can't let go.

Walk to Trout Pond

So I hike to the middle of things
part-way to my destination, as if
I knew where that could be, starting off
on an easy incline, just a mile, late morning
on a sunny early September day,
the dog running ahead, stopping from time to time
to check our whereabouts, knowing how far
she can go before I'll tug the invisible lead
to keep her connected as I walk up
the gradual but insistent incline, sun shafting
into shady spaces in the deep green late
summer forest until the pond shows through the trees
like a blue sky—and then I'm there,
things splicing together unexpected
as years ago I dashed across the thin point
of Cape Cod to see sunset on the bay beach
and moonrise over open sea, full tide—
both paths within the same half-hour spangling
their gold shimmer over separate waters,
one arc setting while continuing to rise—
remembering that night all my life since
and perhaps from now, too, this midday unforeseen
seeing, goldenrod splashed through the undergrowth,
fringes of pond shore melting orange-red,
seasons blending as the gift falls to me, the dog,
and a small silent loon unusual in these parts.

Northern Swim, Late September

Summer made you stronger.
Today on your mountain, goldenrod
and thready asters edge the road,
the forest floor a blaze of ferns.
The cinnamon scent of undergrowth
turning. We lie on the dock like toads
waiting for sporadic sun to warm us,
impulse to sweep aside good sense
until we jump in exulting *It's cold!*
and then *It's not too cold!*
Surprisingly warm lake water.

Up at your cabin the feeder hangs
where the bear ripped it apart again.
The scraggly garden has doled out
vegetables all summer, kale and parsley
still, a dangle of tomatoes.
You rest in the sun. You touch
on how you'll manage through winter,
its frost-claws when you let the dog out
down the slick porch steps,
its companionable grumpiness
more to reckon with now.

Doors to the Pavilion

So heavy, the entry.
The weak with canes
cannot manage it.

The revolving door.
They wait for someone to come,
push it for them.

The elevator door
so massive,

closes too soon.

The bathroom door
wide for a wheelchair but
hard to pull open,
pull shut,

twist the big lock into place.

So far to reach
from the faucet to
the paper towels.

A long walk,
coffee machine to appointment desk

a long walk from the door for exams

to the door for treatments
at the far other end.

Each of the women sits waiting
for someone to open a heavy door

and call her name.

Spring in Manhattan, 1947

Though newlyweds they weren't kids.
My mother took the subway back and forth
from the clinic to her practice on Central Park West,

my father studied in Morningside Park
for his American boards, to doctor in New York
after serving overseas. While they waited for me

she kept working, just starting to show, expecting
with war over the world would turn hopeful.
Meanwhile a couple rode a bus from Mexico

sightseeing along their way home to Maine
when the man took sick in their midtown hotel.
Surprise diagnosis: smallpox—

in just days the City rushed enough serum
and broadcast throughout the Boroughs
Be sure, be safe, get vaccinated!

Snow-dusted streets or warm April sun
lines formed up and down city blocks—
in clinics, schools, union halls, fire stations

everyone agreed to pull up their sleeves
or even their skirt hems for the needle,
my mother and father in line among them.

Hundreds contact-traced right in the City
and back along the bus route to 29 states—
five million vaccinated the first two weeks,

6,350,000 in only a month.
The Killer That Stalked New York
stopped dead in its tracks. A lifetime ago.

End of March, 2020

"They also serve who only stand and wait."

Milton's preachy line comes back to you.
What it meant when you were young?
You were blind to his blindness and the light
he sought. Seemed an excuse to shirk,
leave the hard work to others, just watch
from the sidelines. Now you see better
what he meant, the light he sheds—you,
one of those who stand aside, wait it out,
keep going on your own, indoors, not liable
to burden or cause trouble, lying to yourself
and anyone who asks if you have what you need
and you say you do—groceries, meds, video chats—
keeping inside what you can't get and can't give,
like all of us now who only stand and wait.

My Son Brings Groceries

You leave the bags on the front steps,
it feels like my birthday, festive with gifts—
coffee, bread, milk, fresh greens

this weird new civic call to stay at home
just because we're old we're told *be helpless*
what if I get sick what if I make someone sick

your father my ex has it, taken by ambulance
from his nursing home to the hospital
where in a previous epoch you were born.

We stand ten feet apart, masks on our faces
we don't hug but talk a while.
Friends would be envious we are this close.
You shout *I love you* as you drive away.

Stay

No need to leave the mountain.
Heydays of June just around solstice,
wildflowers by the thousands
speckle the meadow yellow and white,
at night fragrance lifts high from the grass
to meet the bulging stars.

You're weeding among the perennials
you sacrifice some to make room for others,
loving the tending though you know
what it will cost in pain.

Down at the pond so much going on,
wild iris have spread this year
all around the rim, a monarch dips
among the petals, an early dragonfly,
tadpoles, ferns, forget-me-nots

no need to leave the mountain
tomorrow for the highway to flatland,
to the cheerful front-desk greeting
then the measured professional tone—
next round of radiation, chemo in the veins—
no, stay where you are safe.

To My Sister in Lockdown

I can't touch you.
I wear a mask, keep the prescribed
distance

stand at your open window looking in.
You know it's me, you always do.
You're the same but not who you've been—
that smile. More like Mom's.
I think of how to reach you.
Dopey with morphine, refusing food,
you hardly speak but mumble some
of your destinations.

Remember, I say, remember—
in case you can, in case I can get through,
the bedroom we shared as kids,
sweet summer boredom,
our games—pioneers, potsy, boys—

then a long too-short adult interlude,
beach walks, pond swims, sidewalk cafés,
ex-husbands, your lovers, my kids

while I see into your room,
you in the cheerfully made-up
hospital bed, your cat and dog
always within reach.

You are inside
I am outside

you reach me your hand, I hold it in mine.

Dessert with a Friend on Facetime

Lick of an image, tongue of a dream,
favorites from the brain's back pantry.
I ask *what's yours?*
You say *butterscotch pudding—*

I ask *What made you think of it?*
We see in the kitchen cupboards
of our minds the little box of pudding,
Royal or My-T-Fine, its wax paper
sack of powder inside. Flick a taste
off your fingertip. Pour into
a saucepan, add two cups of milk.

Eggbeater, remember that too,
one hand holds the handle
one hand turns the wheel—

we laugh while we imagine how
the pudding heats, its fragrance
while it bubbles and thickens
until of all possible cravings
it's the one to tantalize
the tastebuds in our minds

> (maybe yours too, dear reader:
> everyone's own butterscotch pudding,
> whether you've ever savored it
> you know how rich, butterscotch-sweet
> spooned warm into your dish)

we laugh at pudding
        —What made you think of it?
from our separate brains and screens
this random treat has come to us

that's lurked somewhere waiting to be craved
as now we do and here it is: warm butterscotch.

Tikki Tikki Tembo and the Pandemic

Just as we used to, cuddling on the couch,
but now we Facetime. On separate continents
we open our matching copies of their favorite book,
the story of two brothers who take turns
saving each other from drowning in a well.
They run through the village, up the mountain,
to fetch the Old Man with the Ladder.

A story for these times—who stays safe
and who will rescue us. The old are most
at risk now, some question if we're worth saving
since we'll die soon anyway,
there's only one ladder for the whole village
and will the Old Man arrive in time?

My grandsons know the book by heart.
Little Chang can't breathe, fallen
to the bottom of the well.
The Old Man pumps water out of him
and pushes air into him until he breathes again

but Tikki Tikki Tembo, older brother, favored son,
is harder to save and takes months to recover.
My grandsons turn their page when I turn mine,
we see the same pictures: two careless little boys,
the village, the river, the overworked mother,
the Old Man woken from his purple dream
who climbs with his Ladder down into the well.

'50s Fourth of July

Our house had a flagpole so we raised our flag
every Fourth of July. Dad ran up the old wool
forty-eight stars-and-stripes, then we sang
the Star Spangled Banner followed by

"O Canada! Our home and native land!"
not ours but Dad's, who was an immigrant
though we didn't think of him that way

since immigrants were poor, came from Europe
and had to learn English, like our old relatives,
but Dad came from Ontario and the War
before he and Mom met in New York

and got married. We lived in our big old
Westchester colonial—three glasses of milk a day,
bedtime books, nature walks, Stride-Rite shoes.

Dad would tell how Mom's brothers hugged him,
showered him with *mazel tovs* at the swearing-in
and Uncle Jack offered him a good cigar
when he became naturalized

as if he'd been unnatural before,
though Dad thought, what's to congratulate?
He'd been a citizen all along, but a citizen

of Canada, he wouldn't admit to second fiddle
but son of a gun wasn't it great to be American,
a privilege we grew up thinking we deserved
merely because we received it.

Home Phone

Back when phones connected places,
every night my father called his sister
or she called him. *I'll just give Es a buzz.*
He'd stand in the hallway to the kitchen,
just home from hospital rounds, still in suit and tie,
holding the receiver coiled to the phone on the wall.
Every night before we sat down to dinner.

It took a few minutes and lasted for years,
all they both needed to know
for the time being. *How's everything, Es?*
Short for Esther, short for how are you really doing,
how's the apartment, are you getting out,
who's been in touch, is that neighbor still around,
heard from your daughters living many states away?
Of the original eight they had just each other,

and my aunt always was. All right.
Barely five feet tall, she sold the gray Chevy
when my uncle died and took the bus alone
to the A&P, the kosher deli, *shul,*
all around Yonkers, as far as White Plains.
She'd been a nurse. She held a steady course.
She called from the armchair in her living room.

A tinge of irritation might creep into Dad's voice
if she kept him on too long. He'd hang up
with a firm click. After he died she continued
the nightly call with my mother,
How are you, Carol?
How's everything, Es?
Fine. Can't complain. The kids?

Ondul

So cold.
I do not understand
the instructions for heat
though Mr. Kim explains
patiently, several times, smiling.
Which button when. On. Off.
I only know smile back, nod.
I freeze. From the window
a tree, dust of dry snow, a bird.
Footsteps crunch on gravel.
My flat is large and bare
and I'm alone here.
Bed, table, chairs, electric broom,
an ornamental chest I can't open.
Two students take me for groceries,
each locks an arm in mine
smiling. Caretaker nieces.
They teach greetings, *anayo, hasayo.*
They teach thank you, *comsameda.*
I learn about *ondul,* that heat comes
through the floor. I learn
to kick my shoes off at the door,
I buy a cushion and move down,
sitting for hours, back propped
by the wall, looking out
at the tree, the bird when it's there,
sipping WellBeing barley tea,
listening on my laptop to New York
a day ago. It will be New Year's
soon, western New Year's.
I'm waiting for you.
While I stay low I stay warm.

The Thing with Feathers

A chickadee slams dead against the glass.
I watch behind the sliding door
then tape up ribbons, warning too late—
don't take what's transparent for what's safe.

Sentimental idiot, mourning a bird since it dies
on my deck, when thousands bash themselves
against skyscrapers or sizzle on power lines,
rush to engine maws—how that trick of mind

kicks in: the face you see awakens you
more than multitudes you know are doomed.
In Italy they lay nets, coat branch tips with lime
for bite-size songbirds. Ortolans, orioles, shrikes.

I think its eyelid quivers, later that it stirs again,
what's the difference whose eye is on the sparrow?
This backyard bird compared to vast migrations—
hundreds of thousands who flicker on the news

trapped in unknown tongues they understand too well,
herded onto leaky boats, blasted in their flight paths,
a babble of cost and price and exile.
Its tiny belly barely lifts, some breath returns?

I go outdoors and reach with a gloved hand—
it panics back to life.

Small Change

The coins trickle out, dollar bills
reveal themselves a few at a time.
I find them in dresser drawers,
desk drawers, shelf corners,
old wallets and forgotten clothes
still hanging on the backs of doors.

You didn't always know what you had,
you'd toss coins into pickle jars
or an antique pewter pot, then forget.
Maybe a small fortune, who'll ever
add it up. For now I must sort
and figure everything you've left.

I keep finding more—singles and fives
tucked in thank-you notes, IOUs
you never got around to spending.
Another surprise—you're laughing—
pennies mixed in a can of nails.

Don't nickel and dime me we'd say
back and forth, splitting lunch, buying treats.
Friends owed you or you owed them,
credits and debits nobody set a price to,
always that way wasn't it? *I'll pay you back*

but did we always? Now I spend hours
pondering what we owed each other
over a lifetime, give and take.
The change is running out, I'm finding
less and less, one more proof you're gone.
If I had a nickel every time I think of you.

License

"Dost thou think, because thou art virtuous, there shall be no more cakes and ale?"
—Sir Toby Belch, *Twelfth Night*

On the continuum between Sir Toby and Malvolio,
riotous or tight-assed, I'm out in the streets
toward the back of the demonstration,
my perch inclined to the shifty middle,
often muddled by where I fall someplace
toeing the line between my brother and sister,
mediating—he the rock, she the risk.

I miss my sister, no one makes me laugh
that way, our bellies quaking like Sir Toby's,
laughing until we cried, tumbling off the couch,
off the deep end, we couldn't even breathe.
Now that this benighted, shipwrecked year
approaches solstice and we'll soon be rid of it,
where are the cakes and ale of 2020,
the happy ending, all of us reunited?

Some wedding last month at a hideaway
in the Tetons, retreat of the mountainous rich,
caviar, champagne, tiers of cake, one hundred guests
in hoarded glamor but none in masks,
while everyone I know has honed to the rules
month after month—waiting for when? Spring?
Summer? Another year? To have some excess
in our lives—cram our cakes and swill our ale.

Sitting Shiva during Pandemic

Everything shut down as you shut down,
your last months weeks in quarantine.
I would have sat shiva for you
spread food on the kitchen table
photos on the dining room table
decades of family, friends, holidays, pets

but everyone who would have come
sends surrogates: emails, cards,
flowers delivered by a van
with Monday Morning lettered on its side.
My son says they left out the *u*.

No flesh-and-blood voices
no embraces to breathe deep inside of
no hands handing me what I need
no taste of real kisses salted with tears

since now no one grieves as we want to
and everyone grieves behind closed doors
everyone's caught the virus
mourning inside mourning
each of us sits on a low stool in a room
the mirrors covered by sheets

Two

Puppy at the Beach: An Arf Poetica

digging   he decides
is fun   the sand churns up
fast   spews-spins-scatters
through his paws
the reason to do it
he doesn't know reason
he thinks of what
he finds himself
doing which is digging

why here? something
smelly good
he finds it   bite
of rotten bit of shell
keep digging some
thing else will show its
self
dig more dig down
       a nugget hugs
some tuck of meat
teethe it   teethe it

too young to know
if what he chews
is dead or lived
seaweed   crab claw
     clam foot
         mussel shred
oyster leaking out
between pursed lips

crouch down my pup
and dig what's hid
sand under sand under sand

Starfish: Why I'm Not a Painter

after Frank O'Hara

Low tide, we stretch out on the ledge
to stare at starfish. Wet, flexible,
they stick the tiny suckers of their arms
to the slippery granite. Today quite a few
though summer by summer their numbers
dwindle. A starfish can replace a missing limb

I forget how, that's why I'm not like my friend,
always asking questions I don't think of,
looking things up. Starfish. Regeneration.
Now she perches on the rocks and sets to work,
first a thumbnail sketch of cove-line,
far low mountains furred with pines.
She paints sky in blue washes, leaving empty
space for the great animals of clouds.

I'm more likely to meander, follow the steel rope
threaded through the eyes of posts fixed in the stone,
absorbing through the pores of my senses,
not grasping facts or not remembering,
just trying to keep track. What it looks like, how
it seems to move, the arm or is it leg that reaches
from the rock to find what will be next to cling to.

My friend takes up her brush, daubs grays and greens,
considers how to make things seem as real
as if you see them—while I muck about in words,
raising one tentacle then another
like some starfish loosely fastened in low tide.

Anecdotal Footnote to a Natural History of Massachusetts, by Étienne Léopold Trouvelot, 1869

I thought perhaps a native species of silkworm could be raised for cloth, so I cultivated worms in the acres behind our modest Medford home. Six years of careful study recording their habits from larva to adult. You may read my findings in the *American Naturalist.*

The War Between the States cut off cotton from the South. Mills and looms slowed in Lowell, Lawrence, Fall River, the factory girls up from their flinty farms had little to send home. Why not invent a pliable tough fiber to grow and weave right here on native soil?

I brought worm eggs from abroad, I am French-born and know of *Lepidoptera* in Europe. I would breed a new strain resistant to disease, hybrid of New World stock and Old. Thus I carried back to Massachusetts

    Lymantria dispar, the so-called gypsy moth.

I enclosed my yard with a tall fence, covered all with tight netting. Years of work, patient work: scientific observation, careful tending of the worms. I watched them eat through leaves, dangle from branches, I saw them copulate, multiply, take to air and die.

Their numbers grew. I, lord and servant of the worms—they my hope, my grand experiment. Then a sudden summer storm, high winds for hours. The netting held. I made sure the netting held. Just one small rip, no sooner discovered than repaired.

Only a few moths escaped.

Backyard

They've found a garter snake—
Cain wants to cut its head off
to see if it still moves. Abel wants to feed it
grass and bugs, find out what it eats.

I thought I'd have to teach them
but they're born with my curse, curious,
roots of the forbidden tree.
My two, always fighting.

> *Let it go! It will find its own food,*
> *leave its head on it may speak to you—*

Look at them—
one on each end of the snake, pulling,
laughing for now but soon
they'll drop it dead and wrestle

first in fun then it escalates—
who got more, who's first,
who started it. Where have they learned?
Adam and me, rivals from the rib?

> *Both of you, let it go!*

I arbitrate like God: threaten, bribe,
male methods tested in His Garden.
Be good and I'll give you, bad—I'll take away.
I've had to learn from animals,

mother wolf, mother elephant, mother robin,
to prod or restrain, and yes
I found another way, entice—
lap, milky breasts, cuddling, kisses—

without them I'd be appetite,
craving just to have instead of give.

They tire me, delight me—Adam spends
more and more time from home—

> *Boys! Leave the snake alone.*
> *Let it go!*

I try to teach them: look for signs,
listen for words. They need to read eyes and lips
and fur. Speak animal and human,
use language, so much harder.

What will happen when they're grown,
when we're the multitudes God promised—

Eve's Daughter

She craved to make—
who? She didn't even know,

conceived of me within, alone,

I'm a filament of her mind
as she is of yours—
don't deny the possibility

though not in the Book I'm real
as Eve, as anyone
who isn't.

Daughter in her image,
not god man snake   the boys she bore
but someone with her cycles, circles,
her own way of power.

Ours

women and young girls
who gave birth to the begats.
         Did you think only what's written remains?

While we lived we had names.

My brothers, the simple son and wicked son—
one killed, one fled—
while I, the wise child, stayed.

The rib's a pliant bone.

She kept me secret,
she'd learned from her mistake,
kept me from Adam, kept secrets from me
for my own good, she said
so how could I know her?

Cleave, the Book tell us—
meaning *cling to,* meaning *split apart.*

I left her. How I miss her.

Other daughters sprang from somewhere
for the sons of men to marry.
Did Cain tell the wife he took
of the brother he killed?

Sometimes I occur to you
        (don't I?)

Morning After

Dr. Christine Blasey Ford testifies at the Kavanaugh Senate Hearing, Sept. 27, 2018

She wants to be helpful.
Sometimes a lock of hair falls in her face.
She pushes it back. She asks for caffeine,
they finally bring her a coke.

The men on the right side question her
through a prosecutor, a woman too,
won't that spare her though she's not on trial,
witness the careful probing, like when a nurse
takes a history before you see the ob-gyn.

She's so familiar to us,
out of her element, feeling her way,
she'd like to be more helpful
if she got more help she'd be more helpful—

her fault, like always, bad timing,
eleventh hour after so many years,
good intentions and bad memories

(the strongest one: the two boys after, laughing.
And what may have saved her:
wearing a swimsuit under her clothes)

as it turns out her help isn't needed,
just slows things down. Gets in the way.
        Case dismissed—here come the Big Boys.

Picture Tent at the Edge of Camp

Photography and the American Civil War, Metropolitan Museum of Art

A kid enters a field tent to have his picture taken.
He borrows a uniform, buttons the brass buttons
down his chest, puts on a soldier's cap.
Maybe he decides to hold a rifle.

He's instructed to rest his neck against a metal clamp
so he will stay ramrod stiff. Light through a roof hole
will hit the plates. If he moves, his face will blur.

He's instructed to stare straight ahead
at the wooden box with its big protruding eye.
If he is new and raw he'll look like any kid
undertaking some big thing beyond himself,

if he has already *seen the elephant* as they say,
his cheeks will be burnt, his eyes will show
a disturbed vacancy.

Others stand around outside, teenagers,
husbands in their twenties, one or two older men,
each waiting to step into the tent

then emerge holding a little shadow of himself
in a satin-lined gilt case he can mail home
to be remembered by.

In the photo he does not smile.
This is for his loved ones, after all.

Belgrade, 1961

Ludmila the Knife slit throats.
Sometimes, wearing black,
she crept up in the dark, sometimes she slept
with them first. She was never caught.
In each group of Partisans, one best killer
who killed Germans for them all.

Everyone still drank, years after the War—
come paycheck and weekend, villagers poured
from the shabby hills to root out townies.
Brawls, vomit, raucous joyless songs,
Bulgarians and Serbs beating each other up
with police piling in, sirens wailing

while the neighborhood boys shoved
into her yard to taunt and cheer—
Ludmila strode in her front window
roaring obscenities, hurling furniture
through the glass, tearing off her clothes.

Open Carry

Strap it on, wind it rounds and rounds,
wear it to the July 4th parade, the picnic, the prom,
the pool, playground, ballgame, skating rink,
carpark, commuter train, bus stop, subway, staff room,
the cubicle, corner office, the street, the park bench,
Kroger's, Walmart, Gas-n-Go, Rite Aid, McDonald's.
Wear it to high school, university, shopping mall,
the movies, the marathon. Commencement, convention,
concert, sports arena. Nightclub, dance hall, bowling alley.
Post office. Of course the airport. Your favorite café.
Oh yes—church, synagogue, temple, mosque.
Go look for the littlest kids in grade school.
Go line up the little girls at the Amish schoolhouse.

Sling it across your chest so a cop won't think
you're reaching for your pocket, won't mistake
it for a toy. Wear it to the protest march
so they can't know you don't plan to shoot anyone.
Wear it in Penn Station like the kids on duty
in their National Guard uniforms. Wear it
to the corner bodega, Ricky's, Duane Reade, Starbucks,
the Unfinished Art show at the Met
where the wall-size woman points a pistol at your heart.
Point it at your hijab, your kippah, your dreads,
your topknot, turban, Mohawk, your shaved head.

Shots ring out down the road. *Keep Out—*
Firing Range—Franklin Township Police Department.

Who will we aim for? We don't aim, we just carry.

Elsewhere in the News

The New York Science Times, Jan. 5, 2021

Instead I'll write about whales, a pod of blues,
a whole colony of them *previously unknown*
swimming the Indian Ocean, reported in the Times
a day before the mob stormed the Capitol.

Enormous, magnificent, singing underwater
a slow, bellowing ballad uniquely theirs

a species whose size did not protect them
when hunted at great cost almost to extinction
but who survived, peaceful from what we know,
travelling unfathomable distances.

Maybe they'll disappear again before we can
interrupt. Deep beneath the coastal shelf,
submerged enough to be their own islands
in spaces vast enough to contain them

blues don't yell slogans, don't invade,
they inhabit their own enormity
and do not seem to throw their weight
beyond their comprehension

booming their *own characteristic croon*
such different music from ours.

Tableau

after Sacred Landscape of Pieter Breughel *by Georgii Senchenko, 1988, Zimmerli Art Museum*

A huge blow-up of Breughel's drawing
from the final Soviet years.
Raw pink shadows brushed thick,
sky that broods the color of pale cheese.
Three life-size peasants loom outlined in red,
otherwise colorless. Robed like grim reapers
they set out straw hives. Shimmied high in a tree
where you barely notice, the nest-thief steals eggs.

Decades later war rages in Ukraine,
missiles pummel the artist's native Kyiv—
blasted landscapes, bombed-out homes,
hive-shaped bundles left in the streets.
The beekeepers have no faces. Blank circles
like searchlights stare from their hoods.

Yom Kippur in the Catskill Mountains

Shots ring out.
Beyond a few acres of woods the neighbors
are at target practice. Old college friends
assembled for Columbus Weekend,
hunting season, peak foliage—and this year
Yom Kippur falls on Shabbos, holiest of days.

Volleys keener than *shofar* ricochet
from many hills. Stabs of headache.
I break the fast with milky tea.
Loud music, dogs barking,
the chuk-chuk of extruded shells.

I came to the *shul* of the woods
to inquire of my soul, its false vows,
empty promises. Crest of the ridge
and the pink edge beyond, sky settling
into end of day on the Day of Awe,
a gibbous moon rising behind stars
sharp as bullet holes.

Gates of Repentance, Book of Life,
it's both hateful and useful
to hear guns on Yom Kippur.

Humanatee

"Because of their reliance on the health of their habitat, manatees often act as a signal of their environment's well-being." —U.S. Department of the Interior

You can swim with a manatee.
They're peaceful, open-minded,

sea cows they graze
underwater most waking hours

more like elephants than seals
with their wide pudgy faces,
prehensile snouts and lips.

Columbus seeing them far off
thought they were mermaids
though less beautiful.

They submerge their body fat
in brackish habitat, propel
themselves slowly along

devoted to bottom-growing seagrass,
once in a while coming up for air.

Their teeth grind down, drift forward,
fall out, make way for new ones
coming in, known as marching molars.

Females weigh more than males.
They have no enemies, don't mind
a gentle human touch.

Couture

Alexander McQueen: Savage Beauty, Metropolitan Museum of Art

Bodice of blood-red medical slides
strung like tassels on a flapper.
Skirt, blood-red duck feathers.

She has no face.

None do,

torsos strapped
into leather, fur,
musculature,
distorted contours
taut over skin.

The body as/is
a prism, prison,
seamless,
our only making,
all its own, all it owns,

loosed to hunt itself,
cornered, a pile of whip and antler
trapped in its casing, bondage of seek and hide,

suspicions no one invents until discovered—
missing arms
caged heads—

fabricate, fornicate

ugliness, beauty

spikes
thorns
shreds

Sea Turtle, Cape Cod Bay

"But as turtles head farther north to warmer waters that are the result of human-caused climate change, cold stunnings have become more frequent."
—Turtle Island Restoration Project

Cold-stunned on Great Hollow Beach
a 350-pound loggerhead barely stirs.
The crew from the Truro DPW
wrap him in a tarp, haul him to rescue

but experts at the Audubon can't save him,
vets at the Aquarium miles away
can't save him. In his dying
he reveals what it's taken to live,

head stained green from algae,
mollusks fringing the scutes of his shell,
carapace crusted with barnacles,
so much life clinging as he ebbs away.

Sea-obese, he had eased his bulk
through the water, thick jaw crushing
the shells of deep food. Now he drifts
in the wide bowl of his body.

He could have lived decades more.

Mandatory Evacuation

Take your baby and your little one,
don't wait longer.
I'm going door to door, I tell you
the neighbors are leaving,
have already gone.

Living on the top floor
won't save you.
The bottled water and formula
stacked on your kitchen table,
jumbo box of diapers in the corner
won't save you.

You'll shelter in place?
The worst will blow over—
the good are spared—
you rode out the last one,
the one before that?

When the trees snap sideways
when boats and cars hurl like soda cans
and roofs rip like fast-food wrappers
you'll wait for help
but no one will come.

Do you think the fist won't hit
because you prepared
for its aftermath?
You'll be left
in the powerless dark.

Come with me now.
You're the last ones here.

Biomass

after an article in The New York Times, *April 19, 2021*

Jean took pride how pushing ninety
she could fill her metal pail with pellets
from a barrel out in her shed
and carry them into her little house

her stove warming all downstairs
while she nursed a good Bordeaux.

She'd learned in France in World War II
to solve her needs—stay warm and fed,
indulge in any pleasure come her way

she didn't live to know years later
the vast traffic in those nuggets of fuel

timber forests combed for scrap,
loblolly pines farmed in quick woodlots
fed to the chipper, trucked to a mill

built in a bypassed dirt-road town
that's shaken awake by dust and roar
as pellet-making accelerates

more mills, millions of tons shipped abroad
where the wood shifts its shape again,
lights whole cities with bits of its soul.

Processional

The sleet turns ice when it hits the windshield,
only ambulances and state troopers push through,
then we resume the silent crawl, twenty miles
of standstill—farmers in pickups, hunters,
Orthodox families piled in minivans,
teenagers heading for the only mall—

we're stuck now, hours of hazard, no calling quits.
Too fast means lost traction, slow motion tailspin,
one more of us culled from the line and ditched

but across the median, westbound is empty
until a huge swan, wings furled or frozen shut,
makes its way along the road's iced center
followed by gentle honking, as first one car
then a few more fall into line behind it
and follow the bird down its own lonely river.

Fox Island Woods

Don't think: roots—
       think sway, whisper, whoosh, scrape,
             magnitudes of branches urging
                   shelter and collapse.

             Don't think of roots
         but artifacts: leaves, leavings—
    needles bark cones nuts pods,
blossoms and fringe,

smooth spiked and furry casings,
       what they burst and shed.
             Go greedy for the visible,
                 don't probe deep

enough to clutch
         what grows
      the other way—

Three

New Savage

What keeps you awake these earliest hours?
We keep watch with you, watching you
scream your invincible scream
fresh from the belly

your mother cradles you as I did her
rocking
        purring
                singing

frantic for the nipple you latch on
in gulps, after a few minutes forever
you calm to swallowing
then slower

lull into milk haze
        takes you back to dreams

I'd forgotten
always hungry
how love is amniotic

That, Then

Then I stepped out of myself into you.
That you, the *you* you were then,
not any of the others, those other you's
and not the me I turned from, into.
Yes—*that* self of mine and *that* you,
our selves then, and that's how I saw you
yourself turning to the point of no return
turning the outside-in of me.
I could not go back then, inside myself,
beside myself, beyond or any point between.
You had me then.

Sinkhole

A typo transforms aperture into metaphor.
Misplaced finger on the wrong key
and see, *sinkhope*. So easy to slip
from hope to despair, from hole-in-one
to gaping pit, sunken meadow,
eye on the doughnut not the whole
enchilada gone down the drain.
Who knows what lies full fathom five
when the bottom falls out. No one counts
on falling in.

On our block not much happens.
Flat and safe. A car goes by, a bike,
someone with a dog or stroller but
yesterday neighbors gathered in the street
where a hole opened two feet wide.
My grandson and I went after dark
to stare down at its empty eye.
He held my hand, intrigued by fear,
its deep mystery.

Public Works dragged a steel plate
over it, set a pickup flashing amber
to guard it through the night.
Don't get too close, young man
the driver warned and winked.
In the morning a bulldozer, dump truck,
paver, a six-man crew jackhammering
wide the hole then dumping in gravel
like packing a wound. They poured
fresh asphalt over it then drove away.
Our sink-hopes sealed.

Rehearsal on the Lawn

Princeton Symphony Orchestra at Morven Museum, 2021

Twelve musicians in t-shirts, jeans, masks
play six feet apart in separate sway
Elgar's *Sospiri for Harp and Strings.*
The chords sigh a multitude of colors
a white butterfly floats past late flowers

the few of us assigned our squares of grass
soak in the notes of afternoon sun.
Soon winter will shut us down again,
music retreat to somber indoors.

The conductor pries the melody apart
to parse its phrases, polish a nuance,
the players weave their fingers over strings,
the sighs rise and fall, unfolding, reflecting

all the months so far and those that loom ahead.
We linger on the lawn past the final notes
as the players pack up their instruments,
the harpist wraps a cover over the golden frame,
straps it on a hand truck and wheels it away.

False Note

I decided to lie to you after all
while I watched the cellist
grimace as she played,
her eyebrows flexing up, down,
mouth twitching its bright swatch of red,
the bunching of her shoulders, twists
of her head, muscled fingers flying.
Was I the only one there
who saw her hand leave the cello's neck
to take a quick swipe at her nose?

I thought if she can make such faces
yet pour out such beautiful sound,
her notes blending with the other players'
as quick looks passed among them,
their six hands fingering many strings
for the sake of practiced harmony

what is one lie—I'm accused of so many—

Mountain Cabin

Each year the bear comes closer.
Maybe not always *the* bear, but a bear,
though everyone on the road calls it *the bear*
and it's been roaming these woods for years,
crashing bird feeders, raiding trash cans,
appearing in the backyard in broad day
so we keep our doors closed at night.

This summer promises ripe for blueberries,
the tight green clusters just starting to plump
on the high bushes where the meadow
merges with ferns and trees. The bear
will want its share, I will want mine.

Today a pickup slowed as it passed me,
a man leaned out to say *There's a big bear
up the road a hundred yards.*
I'm only going to the first turn, I said—
Then you should be all right.

Each year I walk more slowly
and today is hard, last night in the dark
pain shot up my legs and bit my heart.
What can I do? I must make it home,
The driveway is close, I'm almost there.
I bought my cabin before 9/11,
not before bears but before *the bear,*

the one who keeps coming closer.
I won't let the bear get all the berries.

Beaver Territory

Dusk—time to see.
I steer the kayak to the bog end of the lake,
slushing slow through weeds.

Gone for two years, they're back,
two new lodges on their mucky island.
I see chewed spikes of trees along the shoreline,
the foreheads of sunken logs

and glide through floating mats of plants,
careful not to tangle my paddle in their roots,
toward a shape bobbing by a tree stump—

I've never come so close—
Head. Body. Larger than I thought,
too dark to read its face

as it paddles in the shallows
scooping green ovals of water-shield
with gelatinous stems into its mouth,

things amicable between us. I see
other heads emerge from shadows.
Dark now, time to stop drifting,
I'll turn back to my end of the lake.

Good Year for Apples

September—a scramble
        up low branches to the fruit

green mottling to red, it's time—

I can reach as maybe not in fifty years—
        balance, grab, tug until the stem snaps

apples never like this!

Summer of 9/11 you came to live here
        those years the tree gave only sour sauce

but now a bounty. I'm back for more:

October—bronze grasses tangle the meadow
        the old tree offers more apples than ever

plumped out, a wild wine-dark,
        wasps swim and sing in the branches

I poke a ladder around below
        find a level spot to perch and reach

a second gleaning, riper than before—
        before the first hard frost

I want to fill the sack.

Breton Cake

There he is—we look out the window,
an albino squirrel in the scurry near the feeder—
while we drink a second cup of coffee
and share a *kouign amann*,

dough interlarded with sweetened butter,
roll fold and chill, roll fold and chill,
each time crease it over in thirds like a letter,
done for hours with easy ingredients

until they turn out to be complicated,
baked with a crust of caramel glaze
like good conversation. Having my fill
in your kitchen again, sipping coffee,

eating pastry hard to find back home,
watching the albino join the fray
who wants same as we do to satisfy cravings
and eats what you meant for the songbirds.

I remember my mother in the nursing home
holding hands with a man in a captain's cap,
neither of them any longer able to talk
but sharing a crumb bun I'd brought from a deli—

such luck, this creature fattening in your yard,
who you expect will stay if you feed it.

Sweet Potato Pie

Thanksgiving, 2020

with marshmallows. The best part
how she concocted it every year
no matter how it came out
the year before. And last year
the last year she made it
she came to the table for a while,
propped by pillows, *listing to starboard*
we'd tease her so we could bear
to see her that way—
the rod and screws in her spine
not keeping her straight,
back sagged like a marshmallow.

Easy to make:
        big can of yams
        small can of pineapple
        brown sugar
        pinch of salt
        an egg or two?

Maybe that was everything, a recipe
leftover from her second marriage,
about all he was good for in the kitchen
or anywhere else, apart from his guitar licks
and repertoire of dirty jokes.
A recipe she knew by heart, adapted to taste,

sweet potato pie, her once-a-year specialty—
we did the stirring, pouring, lifting—
she the slapdash vegetarian
who wouldn't eat anything with eyes
still filled her plate: stuffing, cornbread,
Brussels sprouts, mashed potatoes,
doubles on pie. All of us at the table.
Delicious, she said, *Everything's delicious.*

Florence Griswold's Boardinghouse

Birthplace of American Expressionism, Lyme, Connecticut

A grand old house, her childhood home
but how rattle around in it alone,
her family gone, no money to keep it?

She loved the views from upstairs windows,
the back lawn giving on the lush-banked river
that rose and fell in changing tides of color,
fields nearby, cattle munching on salt hay—

one by one they came by rail up from the City
and rented rooms, having heard how the light lifted,
tidal shifts played shapes on the horizon,

Hassam, Metcalf, others, one summer to the next
would drink their breakfast coffee on her porch
then pile into the wagon and set off for the dunes.

The French were painting *en plein air,* why not here?
The new folding easels, pigments in metal tubes—
artists could work in all varieties of light
and paint not exactly what they saw.

Their ideas, egos, breakthroughs, parlor games—
Florence presided, artful choreographer
providing space for fresher prospects, novel scenes
away from their boilerplate city studios,

she served good food, heady conversation,
kept her garden drenched in flowers,
hung their paintings for sale in the front hall.

Of Two Minds

Listen to me when I talk to you.
Lying here inseparable
sometimes I don't know you—

who do you think you are?
It's easier to write of someone
else, but you creep in
and it's always You, you, yuuu

more than kin, kind of kind—
do you like me, are you like me,
what are you like?

Yesterday at the museum
the handwriting under the glass
wobbled before my eyes
and I felt you slip away.
Where were you off to?

What synapses, sudden lapses,
gaps and precipices fuse us
into so many different I's and you's
urging my brain to chew, to choose

Ma semblable ma soeur
let's try to love each other
as we sometimes do.

We sit opposite at the café table—
who faces into the room,
who faces wall or window?

Leave me alone. Leave I alone.
Don't you leave me.

Snowstorm

We felt it was bound to happen.
With the first faint flakes
I walked a long way through the streets
on both sides of the thoroughfare
and met no one.

By the time I got home
snow came slapping me in the face

it seemed to have a sense of purpose
I have been lacking.
I was in for it now, as other storms
of my decades, but this
ending the hardest year so far

for everyone—storm-breath threats,
bleakness we huddle beneath,
sleet pinging the roof, clicking at windows
trying to slither in.

Before daylight a plow goes down
our invisible street.

The Do Rights at the World of Beers

You belt tunes
                              into the cavern of drinkers and shouters

it's early, maybe the crowd will loosen up, meanwhile
         the sound
system's off   and something else

         (five hundred kinds of beer,
         (a dozen teams tackle the wide-screens)

                              groove eludes
         the eight of you, Black and white
no longer kids—   not quite tonight in sync—
              blurtsy notes and plunderous drums

I've heard you play your guitar like heart muscle
         leap its strings   step the pedal to moonlight

              but tonight's not
         like that
tonight it's hustling for cash

                   keep playing   passing the solo
blazing up   fading out
         who's listening   does it matter?
                   keep the beat, come in on cue, work the moves, lay down chords

         (scan the screens, check the scores)

your chops on automatic,
         not every time's the first time,
comes and   goes
         for now skill beats out thrill
                   keeps you good   keeps you playing
(not the money)   it can happen
                   any time   maybe   next time
even this time

                   you know when the music hits sonic
                   your guitar will kiss the walls

I Don't Know

if my love will claim
more of me than I have
to give anyone in this world
or the next. I don't know
if there is any next.
I don't know if my son is right
saying more women voted
for Trump than Biden
or if Benadryl I take to help me
sleep causes dementia
or if that line break works
or calls attention to itself.
I don't know if falling asleep
while I read or write
means depression or dementia
or too little sleep. I don't know
what we'll do for the holidays
I don't know who I know
will get covid or how sick
or why people don't wear masks
since don't we all wear masks
pasted to our faces.
I don't know about galaxies,
black holes, how to drain pipes
for the winter, how to repair
a screen or infected hangnail.
When I'll see my daughter and grandsons.
How to draw a face or my love's face or my own.

The Gift

You left all this to me

rundown cabin up a mountain
share of lake, the dock

the final dip and rise
the almost-hidden driveway

bronze ferns carpeting the woods
past the wildflower lawn

you left me
to all this

invisible frogs belting
syncopated night-songs

smells of a small tough garden
blueberries for the taking

lake dapples, lapping ripples
colors bending into water

you left this
what am I
to do with it

The Olallieberry

is succulent, hardy, a mix of varieties—
blackberry crossed with raspberry,
blackberry with loganberry, youngberry—

different than the strains it's bred from,
not better but just as luscious
to the tongue, the chew of seeds inside
dark little beads of juice.

We're dining at Linn's restaurant
on the Central Coast of California—
the opposite side of the country
from our home in Central Jersey—

where the olallieberry
though first developed in Oregon
does well on these vibrant slopes

among the hundreds of vineyards,
their many grape varietals pressed
into syrahs, rieslings, zinfandels,

and what are you and I made from
going back even a few generations
as we sit over our last sips of wine
with one plate and two forks

and a warm slice of olallieberry pie.

Acknowledgments

My thanks to the following journals and anthologies:

Adanna: "Eve's Daughter"
Blueline: "Northern Swim, Late September," "Fox Island Woods,"
  "Mountain Cabin," "Beaver Territory," "Good Year for Apples"
Canary: "Snowstorm"
Connecticut River Review: "Sea Turtle, Cape Cod Bay"
Cool Women Anthology: "Ondul" (v. 5), "Eve's Daughter" (v. 6)
Crab Orchard Review: "Breton Cake"
Earth's Daughters: "Belgrade, 1961"
Familiar (Finishing Line Press): "Walk to Trout Pond"
Fourth River: "Ondul"
The Healing Muse: "Bucket List," "Doors to the Pavilion"
Hole in the Head Review: "Sweet Potato Pie"
New Brunswick Free Public Library Anthology: "Dessert with a Friend
  on Facetime"
Paterson Literary Review: "To My Sister in Lockdown," "Home Phone"
Presence: "End of March, 2020," "Yom Kippur in the Catskill Mountains"
River Heron Review: "Tableau"
US1 Worksheets: "'50s Fourth of July," "The Thing with Feathers," "License,"
  "Sitting Shiva during Pandemic," "Processional," "Sinkhole"
Westchester Review: "I Don't Know"

My gratitude to dear poet friends for their critique, support, and comradeship. Thank you, Cool Women, Five Friends Poets, DVP/US1 Poets, and the wonderful students in my poetry class at the Osher Lifelong Learning Institute of Rutgers University. Special thanks to Ilene Millman and Enriqueta Carrington, and to Ellen Foos, my publisher at Ragged Sky Press.

Maxine Susman was born in Manhattan and grew up in Mt. Vernon, NY, eventually settling in Central New Jersey. As professor of English at Rutgers and Caldwell Universities and an exchange professor at Duksung Women's University in Seoul, Korea, she has taught students at all levels, from many backgrounds, and from all parts of the world. For the past ten years she has taught poetry writing at the Osher Lifelong Learning Institute of Rutgers University, receiving its Distinguished Teaching Award.

Her poems are published in several dozen journals and anthologies, among them *Fourth River, Canary, Blueline, The Healing Muse, Presence,* and *Earth's Daughters,* winning nominations for the Pushcart Prize and awards from the Allen Ginsberg Poetry Contest and elsewhere. Many of her poems are set in the Catskill Mountains, Maine, and Outer Cape Cod, as well as closer to home. They often tell about individuals finding their personal place in history; *My Mother's Medicine,* her previous book, relives her mother's story of graduating from medical school in the 1930s, when few women became doctors.

She writes about states of body and mind, art, and people among other creatures in the more-than-human world. *Northern Swim* is her eighth book.

www.ingramcontent.com/pod-product-compliance
Lightning Source LLC
Chambersburg PA
CBHW021024090426
42738CB00007B/899